W9-CHG-198

PRESENTED TO:

FROM:

DATE:

*He tends his flock like a shepherd: He gathers
the lambs in his arms and carries them close to his heart;
he gently leads those that have young.*

ISAIAH 40:11

JESUS, *this isn't how I imagined my life would be, but I trust you to guide my steps, to guard my words, to strengthen my heart, to be the rock upon which I build my family.*

Being a single parent is one of the hardest and noblest endeavors you will ever undertake.

And aren't you tired of everyone telling you that?

Well-meaning friends say, "I don't know how you do it." And you sound like a Nike ad when you reply, "You just do it."

Their comments do hold truth, however. Single parenting is difficult. What two parents often struggle to accomplish you must do alone. But single parenting is also a rare privilege. You are called to a meeting place with the Lord. He wants to help you and your children, no matter how you came to be here.

*Here* is a point of intimacy with God. You are not alone. He wants to be a husband to you and a father to your children. Accept him, pray to him, thank him, trust him. Through him, you can have your best life.

# Day 1: Here We Are

*A father to the fatherless, a defender of widows,*
*is God in his holy dwelling.*
*—Psalm 68:5*

MAYBE THE MARRIAGE YOU believed would last a lifetime has ended. Maybe you never wed. Or maybe you reached out in love and took in a child. Whatever route has led you to this place, here you are—a single mom.

*Here* can be a very good place—or a very bad one. It can be a place of intense sadness or a place of singular joy. You have likely experienced moments of both.

"Single parenting is like riding a bullet train," explained a single mom, "but there's no conductor calling your stop. There's no getting off or even resting."

Honor® is an imprint of
Cook Communications Ministries, Colorado Springs, CO 80918
Cook Communications, Paris, Ontario
Kingsway Communications, Eastbourne, England

40 DAYS TO YOUR BEST LIFE FOR SINGLE MOMS
© 2006 by Honor Books

All rights reserved. No part of this book may be reproduced without written
permission, except for brief quotations in books and critical reviews. For information, write Cook Communications Ministries, 4050 Lee Vance View,
Colorado Springs, CO 80918.

Manuscript written by Lora Schrock
Interior photo © Pete Holiday
Interior Design: TrueBlue Designs, Sandy Flewelling
Cover Design: BMB Design

First Printing, 2006
Printed in the United States of America

2 3 4 5 6 7 8 9 10 Printing/Year 11 10 09 08 07 06

Unless otherwise noted, all Scripture quotations are taken from the HOLY
BIBLE, NEW INTERNATIONAL VERSION®. Copyright © 1973, 1978, 1984
International Bible Society. Used by permission of Zondervan. All rights
reserved.

ISBN 1-56292-708-6

# FOR SINGLE MOTHERS

*Inspiration and Motivation for the Seasons of Life*

COOK COMMUNICATIONS MINISTRIES
Colorado Springs, Colorado • Paris, Ontario
KINGSWAY COMMUNICATIONS LTD
Eastbourne, England

# Day 2: Your Relationship with God

*For God so loved the world that*
*he gave his one and only Son,*
*that whoever believes in him*
*shall not perish but have eternal life.*
*—John 3:16*

SINGLE MOMS HAVE THE responsibility of shepherd-
ing their families in the faith without a helpmate. Is this
ideal? No, but it's real life, and you need to teach your children about the Lord and be an example for them.

God desires to have an intimate love relationship with
you. Are you at a place spiritually where you can meet him?

Do you have a strong, growing faith? Praise God for his
grace and mercy. Ask him to guide your kids' footsteps in

their faith walk. Seek out ways to help others find the joy that you know.

Do you believe in God, but you have let problems stemming from single parenthood block you from a vibrant faith? Get plugged into a community of believers who can help you grow as a Christian. Finding a church with a good single-parents program is a plus but not a necessity. You need to be fed spiritually and work through all the obstacles that keep you from becoming who God wants you to be.

Do you know God at all? Single mom or not, you need Jesus. If you don't know Jesus personally, find a Bible-teaching church and talk to someone there. If the prospect of this sounds too intimidating, visit a Christian bookstore and ask for some resources. It's likely that someone working at that store can share the gospel with you. It doesn't really matter how you hear about Jesus as long as you do. When you're ready to accept Christ, it is a personal moment between you and him. But after you take that step, find a mature Christian to mentor you.

Do you want to have the best possible life? Accepting Christ is the first step.

DEAR JESUS, *you are my rock and my deliverer. In you do I believe.*

# Day 3: Equipped for the Fight

*Do not be afraid; do not be discouraged.*
*Go out to face them tomorrow,*
*and the LORD will be with you.*
*—2 Chronicles 20:17*

JENNY HAD HAD QUITE enough, thank you. Her four children, all under the age of eight, had spent the morning alternately crying, sulking, or wreaking general havoc around the house. She doubted a professional nanny, a police officer, or even a psychiatrist could help restore order.

"I'm not doing this anymore!" she yelled at no one in particular and walked out to the backyard.

"Hello, neighbor!" Mr. Gordon called from where he was trimming a hedge.

"Would you like to adopt my kids?" Jenny asked, half-jokingly. "I'm done fighting them. They outnumber me!"

Mr. Gordon walked toward her. "Have I ever told you about King Jehoshaphat?"

She shook her head with a smile. The former Bible teacher always had an endless supply of stories. "Who was that?"

"A king of Israel. He faced a vast army, one so large there was no way his people would survive. Every man, woman, and child sought help from the Lord. The Spirit of the Lord spoke through one man, who had a startling message for the people: You don't have to fight! They were to take up their positions, stand firm, and watch the deliverance God would give them.

"Early the next morning," Mr. Gordon continued, "Jehoshaphat and his men went to battle, singing and praising God, but they didn't have to engage the enemy. The Lord had already defeated that army."

"So, you're saying I need to be equipped for the battles I face—even those with my kids—but that ultimately the battle belongs to God," Jenny said.

"And being equipped means preparing, praying, and praising him," Mr. Gordon said.

DEAR LORD, *some days I don't want to be a single mom. But I rejoice in knowing the battle is yours. Forgive me when I try to do too much on my own.*

# Day 4: God's Promises

*Surely God is my salvation;*
*I will trust and not be afraid.*
*—Isaiah 12:2*

"IAN'S FATHER WASN'T THE man I should have had a child with. He was into drugs, alcohol—still is. But I was pretty wild then too." Kimberly smiled brightly as she took a sip of coffee. "Isn't it great that God was looking out for me before I was even saved?"

Gina returned her smile. "God loves you and Ian a lot."

"I'm not saying that life isn't hard. Just last week I said, 'Jesus, you know we don't have enough money for the bills. But I'm trusting in you.' And he led me to another part-time job that fits perfectly with my class schedule and Ian's day care. Then, on top of that, I got an unexpected check in the mail."

"Your faith is really an inspiration."

"It's not me, it's Jesus. And why worry about money?" Kimberly quickly pulled a pocket-size Bible from her purse. "Matthew 6:33 says, 'But seek first his kingdom and his righteousness, and all these things will be given to you as well.'"

"Isn't God cool?"

You may not have Kimberly's zeal and unwavering trust—but don't you wish you did? Maybe you've been so hurt or disappointed that it's hard to believe the Bible's promises. However, because these are God's promises and not man's, you can believe them.

LORD GOD, *people important to me have let me down. I want to believe in your promises and obey your commands. I'm struggling to trust you; please help me in my unbelief.*

# Day 5: In God We Trust

*Those who trust in the LORD are like Mount Zion,*
*which cannot be shaken but endures forever.*
*—Psalm 125:1*

MOSES SPOKE WITH GOD through a burning bush, observed countless miracles, and witnessed God deliver the Hebrews out of slavery. Why, then, did he not trust the Lord to provide water? Why did he take matters into his own hands? (See Num. 20:9–11.) Because he was human.

Elijah confronted King Ahab, Queen Jezebel, and all the people as worshippers of false gods. Why, then, did he not trust God for protection when his life was threatened? Why did Elijah run away? (See 1 Kings 19:3.) Because he was human.

Peter sat under Jesus' teachings. But when Jesus told Peter to come join him on the lake, the disciple became afraid when he saw the wind. "Immediately Jesus reached out his hand and caught him. 'You of little faith,' he said. 'why did you doubt?'" (Matt. 14:31). Because he was human.

If the disciples—those great men of God—faltered during moments of weakness, it shouldn't come as a surprise when we do too. No matter how many times God remains true to his word, we still wonder if he'll come through the next time. Christians are more like doubting Thomas than we care to believe.

Maybe we doubt because we think God is like us in temperament. But that's not true. God isn't moody. He won't change his mind if he is "having a bad day." He is the same today as he was at the beginning of time. The promises we read in the Bible still hold true for us. Humans are fickle creatures; God is not.

What is in your life today that you don't trust God with? Finances? Health issues? Your children's future? Where you will be in five years? These life circumstances aren't bigger than our Lord. Have faith to step out of the boat like Peter did and walk into our Lord's waiting arms.

THANK YOU, GOD, *for remaining the same for all time. Your promises never change. I want to trust you with every part of my life.*

# Day 6: Accepting God's Love

*And my God will meet all your needs*
*according to his glorious riches in Christ Jesus.*
*—Philippians 4:19*

MICHELLE STARED AT THE crisp fifty-dollar bill in the greeting card. It was the second such anonymous gift she had received so far that year. She quickly looked up at her coworkers as they went about their business. One of them had to be her benefactor.

"Mary," she whispered, "who left this here for me?"

The receptionist shook her head. "I don't know. It was on my chair when I got back from lunch. I called you straight away."

Michelle confided in hushed tones to the older

woman about the money. A smile blossomed across Mary's face.

"Just accept it," she said.

Michelle shook her head. "I was going to have to use the credit card to pay for groceries this week. Now, I won't have to. I have to thank this person."

"When my husband was stationed overseas, I hit some rough patches. Someone in my church sent me money," Mary recounted. "I asked my pastor if he knew who had done this kindness, but he said, 'If the person wanted you to know, he or she would've signed the card.'

"God is using this person to do his work. I'm sure whoever it is feels blessed to be helping you. Just accept it and give thanks."

Have you ever had someone freely offer to help you? How did you react? Did you feel embarrassed? Were you choked up? Or did pride prevent you from accepting the gift?

People often want to help single moms. Don't be afraid to accept their generosity. You didn't earn or deserve Christ's sacrifice on the cross, either. Do you accept that gift?

JESUS, *when someone offers to help me, I feel like I don't deserve it. Help me to see it for what it is: an expression of your continuing love for me.*

# Day 7: A Place Where We Belong

*Train a child in the way he should go,*
*and when he is old he will not turn from it.*
*—Proverbs 22:6*

IT'S BEEN SAID THAT one of the loneliest times of the week is Sunday morning. That's especially true for single moms.

Many churches don't know what to do with single parents. When I first divorced, my small church tried to include me in its young-singles program, but with a small child in tow I didn't fit in. I then joined a class for parents of young children; however, I didn't belong there either. My classmates were all married.

Next I attended a large church with a single-parent

outreach. For years, the class leadership tried to put its arms around this large, diverse group but ultimately couldn't meet everyone's needs. The only common denominators single moms share are gender and marital and parenting status. That's not a lot of information to base a ministry on, but often it's all churches have.

Finding a church home for you and your children is crucial. You and they need to grow as Christians. You need to hear the Word of God taught and to receive encouragement for the week ahead. Your children need a strong biblical foundation and good Christian friendships.

Perhaps you—like Goldilocks—have found a church that is "just right." If so, praise God for your spiritual nurturing. But if you are searching for where you and your kids belong, find a few churches you'd like to visit. Learn what each one believes. Even if a special class for single parents isn't offered, can you join another class or small group that will feed you spiritually? Is the children's program sensitive to kids from one-parent homes? Are the members caring and friendly? Do you have a sense of welcome or of being an outsider? Pray about this important decision and listen for God's leading.

JESUS, *I want to worship with other believers, but I haven't found where you would have me and my family to attend. Hear my cry to find a church home that honors you.*

# Day 8: The Bonds of Fellowship

*Let us not give up meeting together,*
*as some are in the habit of doing,*
*but let us encourage one another.*
*—Hebrews 10:25*

BARBARA STARED AT THE paint cans in her garage, each one a varying shade of purple. There was no way she could create the perfect color and have Lily's room painted before her daughter returned from summer camp.

Beep-beep-beep. Barbara whirled around to see a minivan coming up her driveway. Vivian, Allie, and Dana got out.

"What's going on?" Barbara laughed as her friends from the Parenting Solo Sunday school class started unloading painting supplies.

"You said you needed help today. Here we are!" Dana declared.

"But I know all of you had plans for this weekend," Barbara said, confused.

Vivian shrugged. "We single moms need to stick together."

"That's right." Allie set down some brushes and drop cloths. "If we all pitch in, we'll have the work done in no time."

Barbara hugged each in turn. "I'd be grateful if you could help me get the right color for the walls. Lily has her heart set on this." She showed them a swatch of cloth.

Allie quickly opened a few cans and began mixing periwinkle with hydrangea, then added a dash of lilac. "I think this is close."

Barbara stepped back, astonished. "I had no idea it could be that easy."

Allie laughed. "I've painted every room in my house. You're lousy with paint but you're good at gardening. Viv is an expert at laying tile. And Dana knows cars. If we pool our strengths, there's nothing we can't get done around the house."

More than any other group, single parents need to meet with other single parents for emotional and prayer support and to combine their talents to help one another. Do you have a group you can fellowship with?

THANK YOU, LORD, *for other single mothers. Let me encourage them just as they encourage me.*

# Day 9: We Are a Family

*From him the whole body,*
*joined and held together by every supporting ligament,*
*grows and builds itself up in love,*
*as each part does its work.*
*—Ephesians 4:16*

IT WAS ITALIAN NIGHT at the local buffet restaurant and Marnie had a buy-one-get-one-free coupon. She built a big salad while Tyler, now nine years old, proudly dished up his own food. He returned to their table carrying a plate weighed down with spaghetti, manicotti, and several other sauce-covered dishes.

"I don't see any veggies there, buddy," she chided him.

Tyler's freckles made an interesting pattern as he scrunched up his nose. "I'll get some next time."

As he slid across the booth seat, their carefully piled winter outerwear slid down to the floor. Mother and son spent the next few minutes picking up coats and mittens.

"What's wrong?" Marnie asked, noticing Tyler's expression.

"I was just thinking," he said. "If we had a daddy, he'd sit next to you. And if we had a little sister, she'd sit next to me instead of these coats.

"Mom?" His voice trembled. "Are we a real family?"

If heartbreak had a sound, Marnie heard it cry all around her.

"Of course we are," she said cheerfully. "I have you, and you have me. We are definitely a family."

Tyler looked unconvinced. "The kids at school have brothers and sisters and a dad. I'm the only kid who only has a mom."

"You don't know that for sure," she said. "Besides, we're part of a bigger family: the family of God. And he loves us very much. Remember what you learned in Sunday school this week?"

"That we're the body of Christ?" Tyler asked.

"That's right. He will never leave us, no matter what."

LORD, *thank you for your promise to be my husband and to be a father to my child. We are proud to be part of your family for all time.*

# Day 10: The Family of God

*May the Lord direct your hearts into*
*God's love and Christ's perseverance.*
*—2 Thessalonians 3:5*

KARYN ADMITTED SHE HAD a chip on her shoulder about the Tuesday morning ladies' Bible study. Although she had never attended, she just knew she wouldn't be welcome into a group of stay-at-home, married moms. However, at the prompting of the Holy Spirit, she decided to go one week.

"Does anyone have any prayer requests?" asked the group leader.

"Bob is out of town again," one woman sighed. "I have to deal with the kids all by myself for a week."

The group murmured its sympathy. Karyn shifted in her seat.

"I'm having a hard time finding the right place to do volunteer work," said another. "With the kids in school, I have a lot of free time on my hands."

Karyn felt her impatience rising when the leader turned toward her. "What about you?"

*I think I'll shock them with a dose of reality,* she thought.

"My job is pretty unfulfilling, so I'm going back to school next semester. My daughter, Keira, has been diagnosed with ADHD, which is hard to deal with on my own. And, of course, no child support came this month."

She waited expectantly to be judged or criticized but instead only felt warmth and support from the other women.

"Thank you, Jesus, for showing me my prejudice," she prayed later. "Our lives might be totally different, but we're all Christians."

You may feel justified in separating yourself from other Christian women, but you could have more in common with them than you realize.

HEAVENLY FATHER, *I have felt unfairly judged by other Christians, so I've judged them unfairly. Let me see others through your eyes.*

# Day 11: Choose Your Thoughts

*Finally, brothers, whatever is true, whatever is noble,*
*whatever is right, whatever is pure,*
*whatever is lovely, whatever is admirable*
*—if anything is excellent or praiseworthy—*
*think about such things.*
*—Philippians 4:8*

DAPHNE CHUCKLED AT A commercial advertising a new face cream. "Do they really think a plant extract will help my wrinkles?"

From the other side of the room, Trevor made a disgusted noise.

"What's the matter with you?" she asked.

"It's … nothing."

"No, tell me," she persisted.

Her teenage son looked over from the computer screen. "It's just that you always have something negative say. About everything. You make a joke, but it's always a downer."

Daphne sat, amazed. She thought she was funny. She thought everyone enjoyed her witty comments. But deep inside she knew Trevor was right. Her comments bit with the sarcasm and anger that reflected her innermost thoughts.

How many times a day do you catch yourself thinking pessimistic thoughts? Or, do all your thoughts tend to be negative? If you dwell on subjects that make you unhappy, angry, or bitter, this will show in your face, your words, and in how you approach life. It will erode your self-confidence. Your children will pick up on your feelings, and they will become anxious or unhappy too.

Discipline yourself to stop negative thoughts in their tracks. Replace destructive self-talk with Scripture or affirmations. Soon, life will look brighter and you will be happier.

DEAR GOD, *I don't mean to think about things that make me feel badly; I can't seem to help it. Help me replace negative thoughts with positive ones.*

# Day 12: No Regrets

*For sin shall not be your master,*
*because you are not under law,*
*but under grace.*
*—Romans 6:14*

IT WAS THREE MONTHS before high school gradua-
tion. Leigh, captain of the championship volleyball team,
had two college scholarships from which to choose. She
was in love with her boyfriend. She had a great family.
She knew she was a lucky girl.

Until the morning the home pregnancy test read
positive.

Convinced that her Christian family would disown
her, she spent that long night crying her heart out. But the

inevitable could only be put off so long, and she told her parents, who reacted better than she had expected.

"I told them Chris and I would get married, that I would still go to college," she recalled, now nine years later. "My mom looked doubtful, saying we'd take it one day at a time. And she was right—my marriage plans never materialized."

A single mom at eighteen, Leigh never made it to college, but she wouldn't change a minute of it.

"Of course, it would have been better if Kaylie had been born in wedlock," she said. "But God knew what I needed as a single teenage mom. I love my daughter and don't have any regrets about having her."

Living in regret is like watching a slide show of your life through gray-tinted lenses. Regrets can unjustly color how you remember past decisions and generally make you feel bad about yourself. Learn from your mistakes but don't wallow in them.

GOD, *I may regret some decisions along the way, but they have made me who I am right now—a woman after your own heart.*

# Day 13: Victim

*Come to me, all you who are weary and burdened,*
*and I will give you rest. Take my yoke upon you*
*and learn from me, for I am gentle and humble in heart,*
*and you will find rest for your souls.*
*—Matthew 11:28–29*

ARE YOU A VICTIM? By all definitions, you may indeed be one. Haunting memories of cruel events or words can still affect you.

Or do you feel victimized by life in general? Misfortunes or bad decisions may have led you to a life you'd rather not claim as your own.

Whether you truly are the victim of someone else or of circumstances, you don't have to live as one. As a Christian, you have power through the risen Christ to live victoriously. That isn't to say the aftereffects of what you have experienced can't color your life; however, these same consequences don't have to control how you see your future.

Shake off this attitude of bondage to the past by asking the Lord to work in your heart and bind up your wounds. If needed, join a support group or meet with a counselor to work through the troubles that hold you down. You don't have to be anyone's victim anymore.

FATHER, *I don't want to have a victim mentality. Only you can restore me. Heal my heart and help me not to see myself this way anymore.*

# Day 14: The Strength You Never Knew

*Ah, Sovereign LORD, you have made*
*the heavens and the earth by your great power*
*and outstretched arm. Nothing is too hard for you.*
*—Jeremiah 32:17*

"I JUST DON'T KNOW what to do." Laurie's tear-laden voice was barely audible in the hushed room. "Gordon said he was in love with someone else, filed for divorce, and moved to New York. But I still can't believe any of this is really happening."

The small group of single moms gathered around the young woman to pray over her. "I know this is really hard right now," Gail said. "I've been there; I know. You will survive this, Laurie. And we'll help you."

Gail did know what Laurie was feeling. She remembered those first shattered months of shock and grief after her husband of twenty years had died. A flood of emotions had threatened to drown her. Now, five years later, she had come out on the other side stronger than before.

Does the church you attend have a single-parent ministry? Get involved! No matter how you became a single parent or what stage you are at, someone is always behind you. How can you help the mom who is struggling with a problem you already have dealt with? Someone is also always ahead of you. What can you learn from the single mom whose kids have left the nest?

"While newly divorced moms may be devastated and find it hard to cope, I think we all learn pretty quickly not only to survive but also to develop strengths we never knew we had," said a single mom.

And the source of that power is the Lord.

GOD, *I need your strength to be a good mom. Thank you for showing me what I can accomplish through you.*

# Day 15: Alone Again

*Why are you downcast, O my soul?*
*Why so disturbed within me?*
*Put your hope in God,*
*for I will yet praise him,*
*my Savior and my God.*
*—Psalm 42:5–6*

DAN AND MARIE HELD hands during small group. It probably wasn't even a conscious thought—he simply took his wife's hand in his. Amy tried to focus on the lesson, but her attention kept returning to those intertwined fingers. That simple flesh-to-flesh connection nearly brought her to tears.

"I'm really losing it," she confided to her mentor. "Next thing you know, I'll be bawling when Rhett kisses Scarlett. I miss having a man in my life." She sighed heavily. "Don't get me wrong: I would never do anything that God doesn't approve of, but I sometimes feel so lonely …"

"God has promised to be your husband," Lynn began.

"I know," Amy said. "But—"

"But that doesn't keep your feet warm at night?" Lynn interrupted with a smile.

Amy nodded self-consciously. "There are times when I wonder if I'll ever kiss a man again, let alone…."

"I'm sure that wanting physical contact is difficult. But wouldn't you agree that what you really miss most is companionship?"

"I suppose. I miss having someone who really loves me, who wants to spend time with me, who knows me inside and out." A stray tear snaked down Amy's cheek.

Lynn took Amy's hands in hers. "The person you just described is God."

God knows your loneliness. He sees those long nights when the walls seem to close in around you and no one hears what you cry out. You may be tempted to rush into a relationship to fill this void, but turn to the Lord first. Let him fill that lonely space.

JESUS, *you have pursued me. You are my comforter. I want you to be my one and only.*

# Day 16: But You Aren't Alone

*Let us hold unswervingly to the hope we profess,*
*for he who promised is faithful.*
*—Hebrews 10:23*

THE SIGN OUTSIDE THE chiropractor's office read: De-stress your life with a massage.

"As if that's all it would take!" Kate laughed as she drove past. She glanced at her watch and punched the accelerator.

She had to get to work thirty minutes early all week so she could take off Friday afternoon for Robert's soccer game. She also had to figure out a way to help Becca with algebra—not her best subject either. Before Saturday she had to have new tires put on the car. And she had to somehow get Joshua to talk to her instead of spending all of his free time sullen and silent in his room.

"Just rub my neck and the stress will just float away," she said as she pulled into the parking lot at work.

Kate's stress quotient had been off the chart since she was widowed nearly five years earlier. She had tried to plug into the single-parenting group at church but couldn't relate to the other single moms and dads. Most of them were divorced and often spoke disparagingly of their ex-spouses. She didn't hate her husband—she loved and missed him more than she could say.

But she could relate to the other parents' stress levels. Like her, each one shouldered a burden designed to be carried by two parents. The pastor had said that no matter how much stress they faced daily, Jesus would faithfully stand with them.

Kate took a deep breath. "Jesus, thank you for being with me. I'm going to need your help today."

I'M REALLY *stressed out, God. I don't know how I will get everything done. I rely on your promise to help me through this day.*

# Day 17: Depression

*My heart is not proud, O LORD,*
*my eyes are not haughty;*
*I do not concern myself with great matters*
*or things too wonderful for me.*
*But I have stilled and quieted my soul.*
*—Psalm 131:1–2*

"WHY THE LONG FACE?" Ken asked me after church.

Because I didn't know him that well, I didn't feel comfortable explaining how I felt. Instead, I forced a tight-lipped smile. "I'm just tired."

"Don't be so down!" Ken exclaimed. "We're Christians; we know how the story ends. Be happy."

*Great,* I thought as I walked to my car. *Now I can feel*

*guilty for not being happy enough.*

I picked up fast food on the way home, but it wasn't until after my shoes were off and I had planted myself in front of the television that I noticed they had forgotten to put the fries in my bag.

*'Be happy'? It's more like 'Be depressed,'* I thought. *What's wrong with me? Why am I upset about french fries? I'm saved. I know Jesus. Why am I so sad?*

Have you ever been really depressed? Have you felt so tired that even getting out of bed is a major undertaking? Have you been so numb that you don't care about once-beloved hobbies? Have you found yourself lying awake, wondering how long it would take to fall asleep?

If you're depressed, it's nothing to be ashamed of. God knows all our feelings—even depression. Seek out help through a counselor or your doctor. And turn your troubles over to the Lord. He loves you.

GOD, *I can barely put the words together to ask for help. I am so discouraged. But I know you love me no matter what I am feeling.*

# Day 18: Confidence in You

*She is clothed with strength and dignity;*
*she can laugh at the days to come....*
*She watches over the affairs of her household*
*and does not eat the bread of idleness.*
*—Proverbs 31:25, 27*

SALLY SNAPPED HER BRIEFCASE closed and turned off her computer. It had been a good day, a great day. The presentation before the board had gone better than she could have imagined. Every question she hit out of the park. Every argument she knocked down with the skill of a prizefighter. Facts and statistics stood behind her like a well-prepared army.

For a moment she let herself dream. What could be

next? A promotion? A raise? A company car? Shaking her head, she smiled and closed the blinds in her office.

"I don't mean to boast, Lord, but I was on fire today," she murmured.

Two years earlier, Sally couldn't have even dreamed a day like this would happen. A new employee, she had survived a bitter divorce and custody suit that left her emotionally and financially drained. She could barely see beyond what the day brought. Always a strong Christian, Sally suddenly felt like the Lord was working in everyone else's life but hers. She had used up all the grace allotted to her, and now she would remain in a permanent holding pattern.

It's a good thing for Sally that God had other plans. She spent time in the Word and in prayer. And most of all, she was quiet and listened. Over time she regained her strength and confidence.

Just because you're a single mom and perhaps down on your luck today doesn't mean your situation can't turn around in a heartbeat. Don't think that being a single mom limits you or your future. It doesn't. Nothing is too big or too hard for the Lord.

JESUS, *thank you for helping me when I ask you. With your strength, I can face tomorrow with confidence.*

# Day 19: Providing for Your Children

*O LORD God Almighty, who is like you?*
*You are mighty, O LORD,*
*and your faithfulness surrounds you.*
*—Psalm 89:8*

IT'S NO SECRET THAT most unmarried mothers live at or below the poverty level. Many must turn to state or federal government assistance. Some may receive child support, but a lot don't.

These moms shop at thrift stores, struggle with bills, and have to say no when their kids ask for the little extras of life. These moms may work several jobs to put food on the table. Money is the two-thousand-pound elephant in the corner that overshadows every decision.

"It's a continual struggle," says one unwed mother. "I keep my head down and plow through, but when I do take the time to look up, I'm overwhelmed. One little setback—the car breaking down, a medical bill—could pull us under."

Are you like the mom above? Then you understand that your priorities have to be in order. You must provide for your little family's every need—physical, emotional, spiritual, and more.

What's the best way to do that? On your knees.

Pray for God's provision—he wants to help you. The Lord promises that he will provide for your needs. He will use you, mom, to do that for your children.

Pray for wisdom in making financial decisions. Ask your church or check the Internet for information on financial-planning classes for single parents. If you do come into some extra money, use wisdom in your spending or savings plans.

Pray for guidance and strength in setting your priorities. It's very hard to tell your children they can't have something that truly is a basic of life—especially if you're carrying around a good dose of single-mom guilt. The Lord can strengthen you to see the big picture.

DEAR GOD, *fighting my finances is an ongoing battle. Some days I win; other days the lack of money wins. I ask for your grace to see that everything on this earth belongs to you and that you will provide.*

# Day 20: The Green-Eyed Monster

*I know what it is to be in need,*
*and I know what it is to have plenty.*
*I have learned the secret of being content*
*in any and every situation,*
*whether well fed or hungry,*
*whether living in plenty or in want.*
*I can do everything through him who gives me strength.*
*—Philippians 4:12–13*

DANA FLIPPED THROUGH THE latest celebrity gossip magazine as she waited for her son to get his braces tightened. Page after page of glossy photos caught her eye. The latest fashions, designer jewelry, fabulous trips—it was like peeking into another world.

She tossed the magazine back onto the table and sighed. Once upon a time, she had known that kind of life. If she tried really hard, she could almost remember those years with Jack as being good. But that was a lie. Their lifestyle had been wonderful; their marriage had been a disaster.

"See you in a month." A well-dressed woman waved to the receptionist, then turned to her daughter as they walked out of the office. "We won't have to come back until after our vacation."

Dana's shoulders slumped. She wanted to go on a vacation. She wanted a new car, a new wardrobe, an attentive man in her life.

"Why shouldn't I have those things?" she grumbled to Allie later that day. The two single moms sat in a quiet corner of a local coffee shop.

"You have a roof over your head, a good job, great kids—and you actually get child support," Allie scolded. "You're very lucky."

"I know you're right," Dana said, sheepishly. "I'm just jealous. I want what other people have."

Do you envy others? Feeling jealous is a way of saying that it isn't fair you don't have that new car, the great job, that wonderful life. You aren't content with what you do have. That makes you miserable—and it is an insult to God, who has promised to provide for your needs, not your wants.

DEAR JESUS, *I often resent people who have more than I do. Forgive me for not appreciating all I do have—especially your love.*

# Day 21: Disappointment

*I consider that our present sufferings are not worth comparing with the glory that will be revealed in us.*
—Romans 8:18

"THIS IS BARBARA. We talked a few weeks ago about you fixing my fence? Oh. All right. Good-bye."

Barbara hung up with a heavy sigh. Bob, the handyman at church, had offered to repair her back fence, which was starting to sag inward. It had been such a relief—one less thing to worry about.

First, he had planned to come by, but his kids got sick. Now he had to cancel because his wife was out of town, and she didn't want him coming over by himself.

Barbara poured a tall glass of iced tea and told herself

it was no big deal, but the disappointment ran like a bitter chill in her blood. It was a small letdown added to a long list of small letdowns.

No one goes through life without disappointments, big and small. But single moms seem to feel those disappointments to a higher degree than other people. Maybe it's because when we were little girls we had grand dreams that never included parenting all alone. Maybe it's because we don't feel adequate for the task of raising children by ourselves. Whatever its source, the disappointment we feel becomes a familiar but unwelcome visitor.

Stop to think about how Jesus felt when he went to the garden of Gethsemane. He asked the disciples to wait while he prayed, but they couldn't even keep awake during such an agonizing time for our Lord. Jesus asked them, "Could you men not keep watch with me for one hour?" (Matt. 26:40).

Jesus knows people will disappoint you. But he never will.

LORD, *I don't think I can take one more letdown. I just want to cry. I know disappointments are part of life. Help me deal with them with grace.*

# Day 22: The Next Act

*"For I know the plans I have for you," declares the LORD,*
*"plans to prosper you and not to harm you,*
*plans to give you hope and a future."*
*—Jeremiah 29:11*

VIVIAN PUT ON HER sweater and stepped out into the cool fall air. She enjoyed her evening walks, although it was getting darker earlier. John and Deb used to walk with her, but that was years ago. Her children were grown now. She spoke to them regularly, but they had their own lives. It was as it should be.

Vivian took the tissue she kept tucked up her cuff and dabbed at her nose. The wind was picking up. Her brisk pace contrasted with her melancholy mood. Although she had many hobbies and girlfriends at church, Vivian harbored a secret sadness. She couldn't accept the fact that she was older and alone—and she blamed God.

In Shakespeare's play of the same name, King Lear had so much inner turmoil that he raged against a violent storm. Do you feel like that sometimes? Like you want to shake your fist at God? We all face circumstances we don't want to accept: illness, financial hardship, grief. More than likely, what you can't accept makes you angry and sad. By not accepting the reality of your life, you're only hurting yourself.

No matter what you face as a single mom, your story hasn't yet ended. You see the current setting and characters but don't know what the next scene will bring or who is waiting in the wings. You don't know the wonderful delights the Lord has in store for you or realize all the gifts he wants to give you. Many more acts are to come, and the author of your life loves you.

FATHER, *I can't accept parts of my life. Forgive me for not believing that your plans for me are good. Help me accept where I am in life and trust you with the rest.*

# Day 23: You're Doing a Good Job

*His master replied, "Well done, good and faithful servant! …*
*Come and share your master's happiness!"*
*—Matthew 25:23*

DR. MONROE SMILED AT young Judi. She was cute as a button, from her freshly scrubbed face to her smocked jumper to her shiny Mary Janes. Judi's mom, Tamara, was a different story. The young woman's glassy eyes betrayed the fact she hadn't slept. Her complexion was dull, her clothes wrinkled. Everything about her screamed exhaustion.

"Tamara," the pediatrician said kindly, "are you taking care of yourself?"

She nodded. "Sure."

"I see it all the time. Young mothers spend their time and energy on their kids and neglect themselves."

Tamara smiled wryly. "I suppose I do that. I just don't have time to focus on me. Judi's dad isn't in the picture anymore, so it's up to me to handle everything."

"Imagine you're a well that provides water to everyone, but no one is filling you back up. Pretty soon the well will run dry, and everyone will suffer." The doctor paused. "Taking care of yourself is part of being a good mom."

To be the best parent you can be, don't let your well run dry. You praise your children, put their drawings on the refrigerator, and cheer them on to each new accomplishment. What if you didn't do that? They would be disheartened. So, treat yourself like you treat your kids. How? Be good to yourself!

Write down affirmations—"You're doing a great job," "You're a good mom," "You're making good decisions"—on index cards and put them around the house. Carve out a spare hour to do something just for you: poke around a bookstore, spend time on a hobby, call a girlfriend. Or, do something bigger—go to school or get more training. The time you invest in yourself will pay dividends to you and your children.

God said you are wonderfully and fearfully made (see Ps. 139:14). He knows your value. Do you?

LORD, *as a single mom, I often feel I'm last on the list of priorities. Thank you for making me a top priority!*

# Day 24: Going Back Out There

*Peace I leave with you; my peace I give you.*
*I do not give to you as the world gives.*
*Do not let your hearts be troubled and do not be afraid.*
*—John 14:27*

CLARICE WASN'T SURE WHAT she felt. Flattered? Scared? Pleased? Uncertain?

"Did you hear what I said?" Damon asked with a short laugh. "I asked if you wanted to go to the movies next Friday."

She covered her embarrassment with a smile. "Next Friday. Movies. I'd love to."

Damon nodded. "I'll see you then."

Clarice waited until he had disappeared around the

corner before dropping to a chair like a puppet whose strings had been cut. The last date she had been on was twelve years earlier with her then-fiancé. Divorced eighteen months, Clarice had thought about someday meeting a man whom she would want to go out with. But now that the moment was here, she was terrified.

She had no idea what to wear. She had no idea how she should act or what she should say. And how well did she really know Damon? What did he expect from her? What would her three children think?

Dating can be complicated for a single mom. You may be going out just for fun, but admit it: In the background, you're thinking, Could this man love my children? Your first loyalty is always to them, and if you enter a relationship, the man needs to understand that. On the other hand, your children have to understand you have a right to go on a date.

Taking the step back into the world of dating, when done for the right reasons, is a healthy move. It shows you are open to new people and maybe to falling in love. Ask God to be preparing the right man for you even if you aren't ready for dating. He wants only the best for you.

JESUS, *I want to date again, but the timing has to be yours.*
*Thank you for your promise of peace no matter what situation in*
*life I find myself.*

# Day 25: Simple Joys

*Every good and perfect gift is from above,*
*coming down from the Father of the heavenly lights,*
*who does not change like shifting shadows.*
*—James 1:17*

TO SAY IT WAS hot and humid that Fourth of July morning in downtown Wheaton, Illinois, was like saying the South Pole is a little cold and snowy. Perspiration dripped off the end of my nose as I spread our blanket near Adams Park. The parade wasn't set to begin for an hour, and the temperature already approached ninety degrees. But to me, the day was perfect.

"When will it start?" My daughter tugged on my shorts as she peered up the street for floats and bands that weren't coming yet. I smiled at her pink sunglasses a size too big for her toddler face, the Little Mermaid shorts outfit, and Barney flip-flops.

"It'll start soon," I replied, sitting down. I took a big gulp from my water bottle and looked up. The cloudless sky stretched out like taut blue silk. The trees behind us buzzed with assorted insects while families safely walked up and down the closed street, looking for an ideal spot from which to watch the parade.

That day is as vivid to me now, years later, as it was that sweltering July day. After a very dark period of my life, God gave me the insight to appreciate such a simple pleasure. And he has given me so many more: watching hot-air balloons make the sky a patchwork of colors; laughing until I cried at my daughter's nursery-school Christmas pageant; seeing the edges of the day melt into apricot-swirled sunsets above the purple Rockies.

Simple pleasures are all around you. Take a moment today to see them.

JESUS, *thank you for the little things in life. Thank you for laughter, for beauty, for kind words and deeds.*

# Day 26: Pray for Your Children

*Do not be anxious about anything,*
*but in everything, by prayer and petition,*
*with thanksgiving, present your requests to God.*
*—Philippians 4:6*

"PRAY FOR YOUR KIDS. If you don't, who will?"

I'll never forget what Fern Nichols, founder of Moms in Touch International, once told me. Of course, I prayed for my daughter regularly, but was I really the only person interceding for her with Jesus?

What an awesome responsibility that is! And what a privilege! To kneel before the throne of our Lord and bring your children to him. But they really are his children, aren't they? You are just entrusted with their care while on this earth. Part of being a good parent, single or not, is to pray.

Does the task seem overwhelming? Not sure where to begin? Begin by studying the Scriptures for what God says about prayer. Then start a prayer journal. Write down what is happening in your child's life. No matter how young or old he or she is, it's never too late for you as a mom to pray. You can pray for your child to have a closer relationship with God, to be healthy, to be safe. You can pray for your area schools, for the teachers and volunteers who are involved in your children's lives. The list of needs is endless, but God isn't going anywhere. He wants to hear your prayers—all of them.

And you'll find that once you start praying, it'll get easier and easier to talk to God. But don't forget to stop talking and listen for his answers.

IT SAYS *in the Bible that you hear my prayers. God, I want to talk to you about my children. Thank you for hearing my requests.*

# Day 27: Traditions

*But I trust in your unfailing love;*
*my heart rejoices in your salvation.*
*I will sing to the LORD,*
*for he has been good to me.*
*—Psalm 13:5–6*

CHRISTMASES FROM MY CHILDHOOD glitter in my memory. I'd help decorate cookies, polish silver, and string popcorn. On Christmas day, we'd open presents in the morning, extended family would come in the late afternoon for a big dinner, then we'd open more presents. Time spent with family; the three-tiered dessert plate loaded with fudge, candied walnuts, and cookies galore; the laughter— all remained precious to me.

During my brief marriage, my husband and I argued over whose Christmas traditions to keep (opening presents Christmas morning vs. Christmas Eve, ham vs. turkey for dinner, etc.). I usually won those arguments because I was terribly sentimental about Christmas. It was too special to compromise.

For my first Christmas as a single parent, I wanted to make the holiday exceptional for my child. We lived far away from relatives, so there would be no big family dinner. I could do anything I wanted to, which was pretty intimidating. Whatever I created for our traditions would become part of my daughter's memories.

I put together different elements—we played a classic Christmas movie as we decorated the tree; we attended a candlelight church service on Christmas Eve. As my daughter got older, we added working at the community holiday dinner and going to the movies.

As other holidays approached, I created more traditions, but sometimes I didn't want to. Those days of celebration often became painful reminders of what I didn't have—a husband and more children.

Don't let feelings of sadness cloud your ability to see that your children need special memories and traditions. Be creative. Have fun. It might be hard to do at first, but what you do now will become part of the foundation for your family.

HEAVENLY FATHER, *I want my children to remember their childhood fondly. Help me create memories to last a lifetime.*

# Day 28: Wise Parenting

*Your word is a lamp to my feet*
*and a light for my path.*
*—Psalm 119:105*

"YOU DON'T UNDERSTAND! You are so unfair!"

LaDonna listened to the familiar stomp-stomp-stomp of her fifteen-year-old daughter, Alexa, pounding up the stairs, followed by the timber-rattling slam of a bedroom door. It had been a long day at work, and the last thing LaDonna wanted to do was fight with her eldest daughter again. But fight they did, this time about Alexa accepting rides with other teens.

LaDonna seemed to hear news reports and statistics on a daily basis about how children raised by single moms were more likely to get involved with drugs, sex, and much more—especially when the dad wasn't around. She wasn't going to be one of those moms whose kids just slipped away before her eyes, no matter how much Alexa ranted. LaDonna always carefully explained her rules to both of her daughters, but Alexa pushed the envelope with each one.

"There are times I doubt myself," LaDonna told her sister the next day. "I've read a lot of parenting books, talked to other moms—but at the end of the day, it's just me. No dad to help make decisions and discipline the girls."

Tonya nodded. "Mick and I balance each other when it comes to house rules. But you've got to stick to your guns with Alexa, because Alysha is going to imitate her older sister."

"I pray every day for wisdom," LaDonna said.

As a single parent, decisions you make regarding discipline are important—and the pressure you feel even greater. But you aren't alone: God is a prayer away, and the Bible, the best parenting book ever written, offers inspired advice and wisdom. Choose to trust in him and his Word.

FATHER, *I need your help to keep my children on the straight and narrow. Help me be firm when I need to. Thank you for the Bible, your instruction and guidance.*

# Day 29: Wild Child

*We do not know what we ought to pray for,*
*but the Spirit himself intercedes for us*
*with groans that words cannot express.*
*—Romans 8:26*

STEPHANIE KNEW SHE HAD her hands full when Dakota could speak in full sentences at eleven months. Her daughter had boundless energy and a desire to explore everything. When Stephanie put her down for the night, Dakota would stare through her crib slats like she was in prison.

The childhood years alternated between sweetness and defiance. The full-on rebellion didn't hit until Dakota turned twelve and discovered boys weren't that gross after all.

Battles waged over small things—forgetting homework, neglecting chores. Then came the lies and missed curfews. War was declared when she entered high school, and everything came tumbling after: smoking pot, ditching classes, coming home drunk. Dakota was determined to live her life by her rules, not her mother's.

Stephanie's heartbreak was palpable. Her angel had turned into a person she didn't recognize or even want to know. Her daughter was throwing away a bright future with both hands—and Stephanie felt all she could do was watch. At the same time, she could also see how Dakota's destructive behavior was impacting her younger sons.

Falling to her knees one night, Stephanie sobbed, "What did I do wrong?"

One of the hardest parts of single parenting teens in rebellion is believing that you aren't a bad parent. After all, you raised them, right? However, the decisions your children make are theirs alone. They are their own moral agents.

At a time like this, you must balance the need to protect the child who is acting out with your other children's needs—and your own. It might feel easier to isolate yourself, but you are vulnerable. Get the help you need and pray without ceasing.

GOD, *I have so many emotions raging in my heart. I want to give up and not care anymore. I can barely pray, but I don't doubt your love for me or my child.*

# Day 30: Parenting with an Ex

*By wisdom a house is built,*
*and through understanding it is established;*
*through knowledge its rooms are filled*
*with rare and beautiful treasures.*
*—Proverbs 24:3–4*

ALLIE BANGED THE CORDLESS phone down so hard that for a moment she thought she had broken it. But it remained intact, even though her composure was fractured.

It was Frank's weekend to take the kids. She had made plans—a manicure, a movie with Barbara, and a long walk down by the river. Now he called to say something had come up, he was sorry, and could she just explain it to the children?

"It never fails," she muttered as black thoughts and angry memories surged through her. Frank had released the tidal wave of pent-up hostility Allie usually kept back. Their marriage had ended with the bitterness of broken dreams. It was all she could do not to tell her kids exactly what she thought of their father.

"But that would only hurt them," Dana said at the Parenting Solo class. "If you cut down their father, it will make them sad and eventually angry with you."

Allie's shoulders slumped. "I'm really trying to work with him, to support him as their father. But I can't separate Frank the dad from Frank my ex-husband."

Vivian chimed in, "God sees what you and Frank do and say. We need to pray for God to give you wisdom to co-parent together—and for strength to do the right things for your children."

Successful co-parenting takes a lot of cooperation and work. It involves putting your kids' needs ahead of your own. Whatever your relationship is with your children's father, God wants you to ask yourself, "What would Jesus do?"

LORD, *I want my children to have a healthy relationship with their father. I know I must do my part to ensure that. Thank you for the grace I know you will give me.*

# Day 31: Parenting All Alone

*Trust in the LORD and do good;*
*dwell in the land and enjoy safe pasture.*
*Delight yourself in the LORD and he*
*will give you the desires of your heart.*
*—Psalm 37:3–4*

IT TAKES TWO TO make a baby, but sometimes only one raises it. Maybe the father of your child is a parent only in the biological sense. Maybe you've adopted a child and never knew the father.

Parenting all alone is different from co-parenting. The good news? You can raise your child exactly how you want without consulting anyone. The bad news? You can raise your child exactly how you want without consulting anyone.

You're the one with all the guilt. You get to explain to neighbors, teachers, coworkers, and even your children why Dad isn't in the picture. You get to sit in awkward silence as they struggle with how to respond.

You're the one with all the responsibility. You make all the decisions, for better or worse. No one with an equal stake in raising the kids is there to offer his opinion and insight. You are the lone parent.

Unless you have family nearby to help, you don't often get a break. There's no handing the kids off to their dad for visitation. When the babies go to bed at seven-thirty, you are in for the night.

But let me tell you a secret—all of these responsibilities are tinged with joy. You just have to look for it.

You get to go to dance programs, spelling bees, band recitals, soccer games, teacher conferences. You're the one who gets to play games, watch videos, spend quality time. Watching your children grow up and experiencing all the bittersweet moments along the way are all yours.

Whether you are parenting with your children's father or without him, know this: You are never alone. Jesus stands right by your side to help you every step of the way.

FATHER, *you know exactly where I'm at in life. Nothing is too difficult for you. There is none like you.*

# Day 32: Advice

*Listen to advice and accept instruction,*
*and in the end you will be wise.*
*—Proverbs 19:20*

DANA TURNED THE ENVELOPE over a few times before opening it and taking out the letter. Her former mother-in-law's spidery handwriting flowed over three pages. The older woman and she had gotten along tolerably well after the divorce, and Dana encouraged her children to send their Nana cards and pictures.

As she read, Dana could feel her blood pressure rising. She angrily tossed the letter on the kitchen table. Who on earth did Jean think she was? She glared at the thick missive as if its writer had physically attacked her.

"I didn't want advice from her when I was married!" she declared at the next Parenting Solo Sunday school class. "My ex-mother-in-law doesn't know how to mind her own business. Who is she to give me advice?"

"People who give advice to single moms need to think before speaking," Allie said with a laugh. "My favorite is when friends give me advice on men—like I was never married before!"

Barbara shook her head. "My parents, who have been married forty years, know a lot about raising kids but know nothing about single parenting. They just don't understand that how they did things won't work for me."

Vivian, who had been silent for quite a while, cleared her throat. "I really do understand where you're coming from, but I need to point out what it says in the Bible. Several times in Proverbs we're instructed to accept advice and learn from it."

"Not worthless advice, I bet," Dana snorted.

"Maybe not. But do we sometimes reject advice out of hand because it's something we don't want to hear?" Vivian asked. "I bet among all the chaff you can find some grain. Look for kernels that can help you."

LORD, *I am not always willing to listen to others' advice. Help me listen to the insights you would have me hear.*

# Day 33: Mom as Mom

*What, then, shall we say in response to this?*
*If God is for us, who can be against us?*
*—Romans 8:31*

I'M SURE YOU'VE DONE IT; I know I have. You've been forced into the uncomfortable mold of being both mom and dad to your kids.

But you can't be their father for the simple reason that you're their mother—a tired, stretched-too-thin mother. Think of all the roles you fulfill daily: chauffeur, counselor, cook, maid, coach, seamstress, disciplinarian, nurse, play-mate—the list goes on. God didn't design you to be dad on top of all that.

Or maybe you're too busy being your kids' pal to be

their mom. A tight bond exists between a single mom and her children. It can be very easy to confide your troubles to your children, hang out with them, and become their best friend. That, too, isn't what God intended for you.

We live in a fallen world, and God's best designs sometimes don't come to fruition. Situations force you to step into the traditional father role. You may have to make decisions that are foreign and uncomfortable for you.

And becoming a friend to your children isn't inherently bad, but you have to remember where the boundaries are. You have to know when to stop being a buddy and start being a mom.

Let Christ be the head of your household. Let your kids' friends be their friends. You be their mother.

LORD JESUS, *I can't be both parents. And I can't always be my kids' best buddy. With your strength, however, I can be the best mom I can be.*

# Day 34: The Flight of the Red Baron

*Therefore do not worry about tomorrow,*
*for tomorrow will worry about itself.*
*—Matthew 6:34*

"THAT'S IT, GREGORY! Run, run, run!"

Carmen watched as her son ran down the hill toward the open park. Trailing behind him on the early March breeze flew his airplane-shaped kite. She had tried to explain that it looked like the plane flown by the Red Baron, a World War I flying ace, but Gregory didn't care; he just wanted it to soar.

Carmen carefully assembled the kite, making sure its tail had enough weight. "This is how you do it, son," she began.

Gregory frowned. "No, Mama. I want to do it all by myself. Let me do it."

Reluctantly, she handed the kite to him. "Now make sure you run fast. And let out more string as it starts to fly."

"I know, Mama. Let me do it!"

Gregory started to run. The kite skipped across the grass until just the right gust caught it and launched it four feet off the ground. Gregory's little legs pumped faster than Carmen thought possible. Up, up the kite went, higher into the sky.

"Look at him go," she whispered. She felt proud of her son's accomplishment—and a little sad.

Parenting is a process of letting go. As a single mom, do you secretly long for the day your children move out and you can be alone? Or, do you dread that day, feeling like the meaning of your life will have disappeared?

Don't spend today waiting for or dreading tomorrow. Enjoy every moment of your children's childhood. Tomorrow will be here before you know it.

FATHER, *I feel sad when my children don't need me like they used to. Help me to see this is all according to your plan, that they aren't leaving me—they're just growing up.*

# Day 35: Empty Nest

*The LORD, the LORD, is my strength and my song;*
*he has become my salvation.*
*—Isaiah 12:2*

VIVIAN PICKED UP THE remote and clicked off the television. Nothing good was on—just reality TV or trashy talk shows. Where had all the good dramas gone?

"Are you hungry?" she asked Patches, who looked up hopefully and wagged his tail.

Vivian walked to the kitchen, the cocker spaniel at her feet. When John and Deb were little, they'd have ice cream during *The Wonderful World of Disney* on Sunday evenings. She smiled, remembering how John would beat the ice cream and chocolate syrup together until it became light brown. "It's frosting, Mom," he would explain.

"Here you go." She gave Patches a rawhide bone. The dog looked at her questioningly, then scampered back to the family room. As Vivian closed the pantry, a colorful brochure on the table caught her eye.

Her friend, Dana, had approached her with information on a gated community near the shopping mall. "It has maintenance-free yards and a community center with all kinds of activities," she had said. "It's worth looking into."

Vivian had considered selling the house and moving to a condo or an apartment, but she just couldn't do it. She had spent her adult life here—first with Bob and the kids, then with just the kids after Bob died. John and Deb had taken their first steps in the living room, had attended the school down the block, had learned to drive on their street. Leaving the house would be like leaving her life.

For single parents, the empty-nest syndrome is multiplied 100 percent. Raising our children, providing for them, sharing our lives with them—it's the focus of our adult years. But when those children successfully fly away, we're faced with an empty house.

Take advantage of this time to rediscover hobbies you

never had time for, volunteer at a local charity, renew old acquaintances, take a class. It's time to rediscover you. And don't forget—your children may have moved out, but they will always need their mom.

JESUS, *I miss my children very much, but I want to focus my eyes on you, and see what's in store for the rest of my life.*

# Day 36: Healing of Wounds

*My help comes from the LORD,*
*the Maker of heaven and earth.*
*—Psalm 121:2*

LOUD MUSIC, SHOUTING CHILDREN, fried food. It wasn't the circus: It was lunchtime at the local hamburger joint.

"Have fun," Barbara called after her daughter, who scampered off to the playland. "Sorry this isn't haute cuisine," she said sheepishly to her companions, "but Lily loves this place."

Vivian took a bite of cheeseburger. "It wasn't that long ago that my kids were begging me to bring them here."

Dana tried to follow the conversation while watching her

two younger boys dive into a cage filled with multicolored plastic balls. "It wasn't that long ago haute cuisine was part of my lifestyle.

"Until I left Jack, of course," she added with a crooked grin.

"Do you miss it?" Barbara asked.

"Good restaurants? Yes. Life with Jack? No."

Vivian smiled. "I'm always surprised how you're able to joke about your divorce so easily."

Dana shrugged. "Time, I guess. It doesn't hurt any more."

The other women nodded, except for Allie, who left the table to find her children.

"I think I just put my foot in my mouth," Dana sighed.

"Your wounds are healed," Barbara said. "Hers are fresh."

Does thinking about your children's father send sorrow crashing over you? Or is it more like an old scar that only itches occasionally? Don't be surprised when other single moms feel or react differently than you. You're an individual who has had a unique experience—how could others feel the same as you do? Have patience when they don't understand your feelings.

LORD GOD, *thank you for friends who try to understand what I'm going through. But sometimes they can't relate. I'm thankful that you, God, do understand everything in my life.*

# Day 37: A Time to Laugh

*Let the heavens rejoice, let the earth be glad;*
*let the sea resound, and all that is in it;*
*let the fields be jubilant, and everything in them.*
*Then all the trees of the forest will sing for joy.*
*—Psalm 96:11–12*

BELINDA STARED, TRANSFIXED. The dress was an incredible shade of sapphire blue with a flowing hemline. It was the type of dress Ginger Rogers could have worn for a dance with Fred Astaire.

"Mommy, buy it! Buy it!" Elizabeth gently touched the filmy fabric.

"Oh, if wishes were horses," she murmured after looking at the price tag.

Elizabeth dove into the middle of the circular clothes rack. "Mommy, you can't see me!"

"Uh-huh," Belinda said absently as she strolled through the department. She needed an outfit for her brother's wedding, which was only a month away. Tom had said he was inviting several single guys, so she wanted to have just the right dress.

Unfortunately, she had told Elizabeth that weddings often brought potential dates.

"Mommy! Buy this dress!" her daughter said loud enough for everyone to hear. "You're sure to get a date with this one!"

I'm not looking up, I'm not looking up. Belinda's face went hot as she focused on a silk pantsuit. Elizabeth appeared at her side carrying something black with pink sequins.

"You'll look so beautiful you're sure to get a date," Elizabeth said in awe. Several women nearby chuckled.

Belinda had a choice: to react in embarrassment or in laughter. She chose the latter. She swept her daughter up in a big hug. "Thank you, darling girl. It's lovely."

Countless times in parenting—especially in single parenting—you can either cry or you can laugh. Choose laughter.

LORD, *help me appreciate the times I can find the humor in a situation.*

# Day 38: Have Fun

*A happy heart makes the face cheerful,*
*but heartache crushes the spirit.*
*—Proverbs 15:13*

PATRICIA LET THE HOT water run until clouds of steam fogged up the kitchen window. She slid the skillet and saucepan under the blanket of white bubbles.

"Mama, can I have water, too?" Sonia called from her play kitchen.

Patricia had "No" on her lips without thinking. She could envision the water and suds splashed on the floor, on the walls. She could see Sonia soaked to the bone in the ensuing mess.

She looked over her shoulder at her adopted daughter. A single woman in her forties, Patricia knew in her heart she was meant to be a mom. Her dreams began to fade as the years passed. Then she watched a TV program on orphans in Romania. Within a year, she had Sonia, and their lives completely changed.

It wasn't all hugs and fairy tales. Becoming a mother to a five-year-old child who barely spoke English was enough to bring her back to earth. Long days of parenting alone left Patricia hardly in the mood to have water all over her kitchen.

"Honey, I don't …" Patricia paused, looking into her daughter's hopeful brown eyes.

Why not? The question echoed in her mind. What will it hurt?

"I don't see why not," she heard herself saying. She filled the small plastic sink with water and gave Sonia a few plastic tumblers to "wash." Some water did spill, but it couldn't compare to the joy and laughter Patricia shared with her child that evening.

As a single mom, sometimes you are so tired, the idea of having fun and letting loose is more of a chore than a pleasure. Over time, it becomes easier to say no than to play a game, act silly, ride bikes, or read aloud. But ask yourself, "Why not?" The time you spend having fun with your children is what will matter in the future.

JESUS, *I want to enjoy my children more, but sometimes life gets in the way. I ask for your grace to say yes to fun.*

# Day 39: Enjoy Your Children

*Sons are a heritage from the LORD,*
*children a reward from him.*
*—Psalm 127:3*

ARE YOU SO BUSY making ends meet that you don't make time to have fun with your children? Does being the disciplinarian make it hard for you to switch gears and play with your sons and daughters? Do you avoid relaxing with them because their idea of entertainment would break King Midas's bank?

Relax. There are plenty of inexpensive ways for you and your children to have fun together. It all starts with your attitude. Tell yourself that it's all right to let loose—and that it won't cost a fortune. Get a deck of cards and some plastic utensils, and enjoy a crazy game of Spoons. Work a puzzle or play a board game together. Go to the library and rent a video (usually free), and teach your children what makes a movie a classic.

In the warmer months, head to the great outdoors, whether that's the mountains, the beach, or the neighborhood park. Take along a kite, a Frisbee, a picnic lunch. Push your kids sky-high on the swings or play a game of tag.

Older teens may not want to hang out with mom. Enjoy your children at this age by hosting their friends over for a game night or sleepover. Help them develop their skills and interests, and see if any overlap with yours.

But quality fun time with your children doesn't have to involve playing. Spend time talking to your children. Find out what their hopes and dreams are. Ask questions, then really listen to the answers.

God wants you to enjoy your children. What can you do today to have fun?

ALMIGHTY GOD, *I worship you for being all-loving and all-compassionate. Forgive me for the times I am too busy to listen and spend time with my family.*

# Day 40: Here We Go

*The LORD is my light and my salvation—*
*whom shall I fear?*
*The LORD is the stronghold of my life—*
*of whom shall I be afraid?*
*—Psalm 27:1*

WE'RE STILL HERE—single moms. We have one of the most important jobs in the sight of God—raising our children to be good adults. The challenges we face change and increase with each sunrise.

It doesn't matter how we got here. It only matters where we go and how we get the job done.

Where we go is straight to the Lord, praising and praying all the way. He isn't a fairy godmother who will make all your difficulties disappear with the wave of a magic wand. He is, however, the Creator of the universe who will carry you while you carry your burdens.

To have your best life starting right now, today, you don't have to wait until everything is perfect because that will never happen. However, you can have joy in the midst of the imperfection.

"Gladness and joy will overtake them, and sorrow and sighing will flee away" (Isa. 35:10). Isn't that a wonderful picture? Don't you want sorrow to flee and joy to overtake you? You can have this joy through Jesus.

GOD, *I don't know what tomorrow will bring. Set me free from my worries. With you I can approach tomorrow with anticipation, not fear.*

*Additional copies of this and other Honor products
are available wherever good books are sold.*

*If you have enjoyed this book,
or if it has had an impact on your life,
we would like to hear from you.*

*Please contact us at:*

*HONOR BOOKS
Cook Communications Ministries, Dept. 201
4050 Lee Vance View
Colorado Springs, CO 80918
Or visit our Web site:
www.cookministries.com*